Rustic Warmth

11 afghans - 9 to crochet and 2 to knit

Whether you're headed for the great outdoors or looking to bring a bit of the great outdoors into your home, these 11 rustic afghans are ideal for beating the chill. With 9 designs to crochet and 2 to knit, you'll find variety and inspiration between these pages. Our detailed, easy-to-follow instructions will help you craft the perfect afghan to bring warmth to any space or gift to the nature enthusiast in your life. The mountains are calling, the woods are calling, and you must go!

LEISURE ARTS, INC. • Maumelle, Arkansas

TABLE OF CONTENTS

GENERALS INSTRUCTIONS

ABBREVIATIONS

CC	Contrasing Color
ch(S)	chins(s)
dc	double crochet(S)
dtr	double treble crochet(s)
ex sc	extended single crochet(s)
FPdc	Front Post double crochet(s)
K	knit
MC	Main Color
mm	milimeters
P	PURL
PSSO	passed slipped stitch over
Rnd(s)	Round(s)
sc	single crochet(s)
sp(s)	space(s)
st(s)	stitch(es)
tbl	through back loop(s)
tog	together
tr	treble crochet(s)
YO	yarn over

★ — work instructions following ★ as many **more** times as indicated in addition to the first time.

† to † — work all instructions from first † to second † **as many** times as specified.

( ) — work enclosed instructions **as many** times as specified bt the number immediately following **or** work all enclosed instructions in the stitch or space indicated or contains exP1anatory remarks.

GAUGE

Correct gauge is essential for proper size, Hook or needle size given in instructions are merely guides and should never be used without first making a samP1e swtch in the stitch, yarn, and hook or needle specified. Then measure it, counting your stitches and rows carefully. If you have more stitches per inch than specified, try again with a larger size hook or needle; if fewer, try again with smaller size. Keep trying until you find the size thst will give you the specified gauge. DO NOT HESITATE TO CHANGE HOOK OR NEEDLE SIZE TO OBTAIN CORRECT GAUGE.

CHANGING COLORS

Work the last stitch to within one step of comP1etion, hook new yarn *(Fig. 1)* and draw through loops on hook. Cut old yarn and work over both ends.

Fig. 1

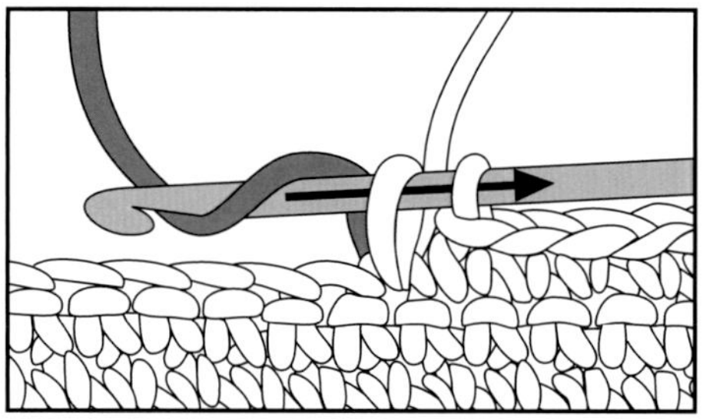

JOINING WITH SC

When instructed to join with sc, begin with a slip knot on hook,. Insert hook in stitch or space indicated., YO and pull up a loop, Yo and draw through both loops on hook.

FREE LOOPS

After working in Back or Front Loops Only on a row or round, there will be a ridge of unused loops. These are called the free loops. Later, when instructed to work in the free loops of the same row or round, work in these loops ***(Fig. 2a)***.

When indiated to work in free loops of the chain, work in loop indicated vby arrows ***(Fig. 2b)***.

Fig. 2a

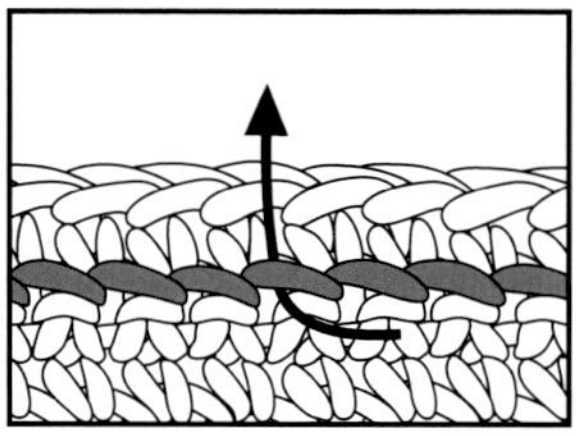

Fig. 2b

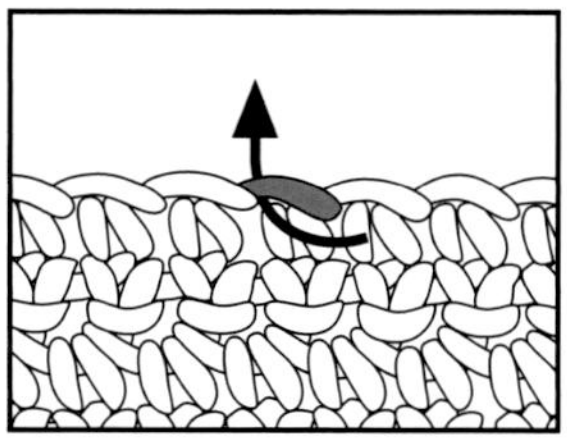

BACK LOOP ONLY

Work only in loop(s)indicated by arrow ***(Fig. 3***).

Fig. 3

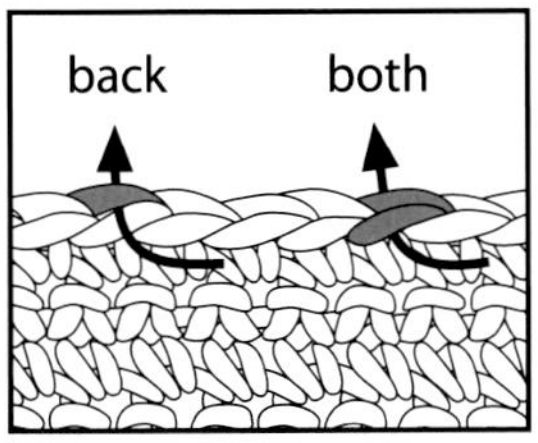

FRONT POST DOUBLE CROCHET *(abbreviated FPdc)*

YO, insert hook from front to back around post of st indicated ***(Fig. 4a)***. YO and pull up a loop ***(Fig. 4b)***,
(YO and draw through 2 loops on hook) twice.
Skip st behind FPdc.

Fig. 4a

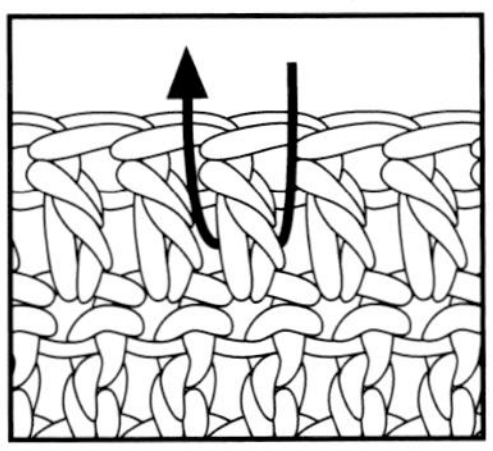

Fig. 4b

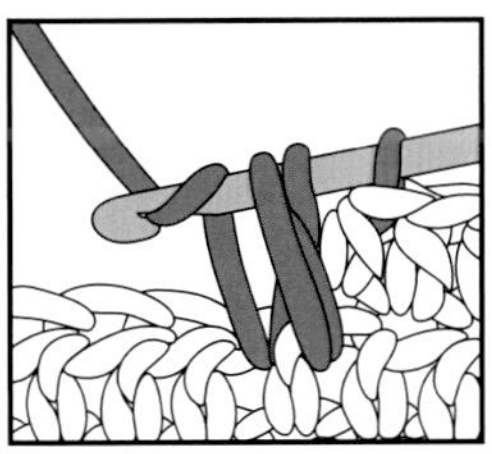

YARN OVERS

After a knit stitch, before a knit stitch

Bring the yarn forward **between** the needles, then back **over** the top of the right hand needle, so that it is now in position to knit the next stith ***(Fig. 5a)***.

Fig.5a

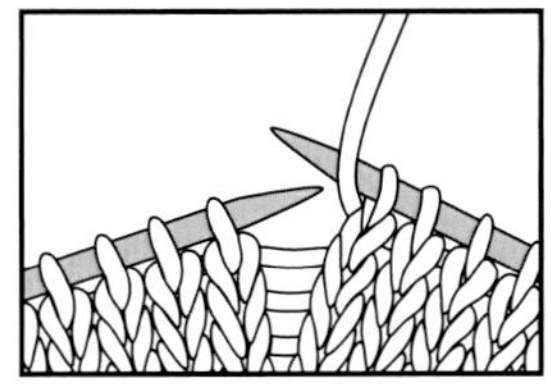

After a purl stitch, before a purl stitch

Take yarn **over** the right hand needle to the back, then forward **under** it, so that it is now in position to purl the next stitch ***(Fig. 5 b)***.

Fig.5b

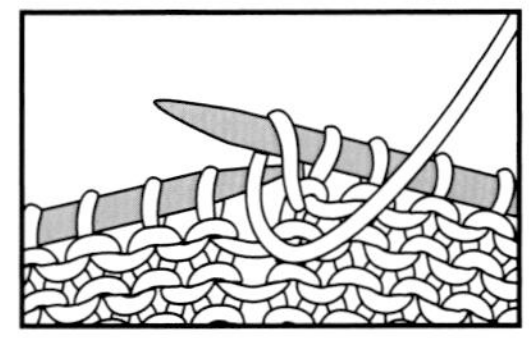

After a knit stitch, before a purl stitch

Bring the yarn forward **between** the needles, then back **over** the top of the right hand needle and forward **between** the needles again, so that it is now in position to purl the next stitch ***(Fig. 5c)***.

Fig.5c

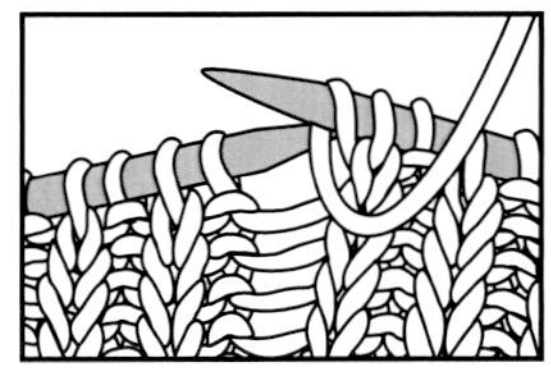

After a purl stitch, before a knit stitch

Take yarn over right hand needle to the back, so that it is now in the position to knit the next stitch ***(Fig. 5 d)***.

Fig.5d

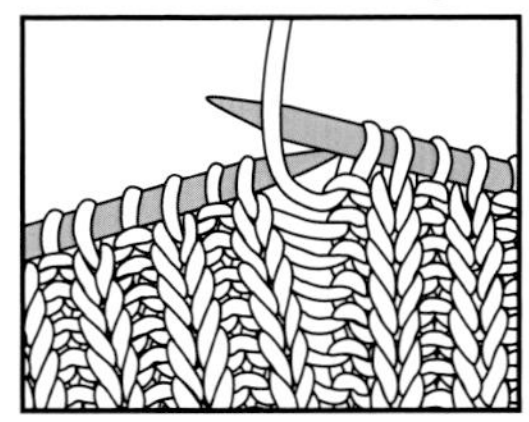

REVERSE SINGLE CROCHET

Working from left to right, ★ insert hook in st to right of hook ***(Fig. 6a)***, YO and draw through, under and to left of loop on hook (2 loops in hook) ***(Fig. 6b)***, YO and draw through both oops on hook ***(Fig. 6c) (reverse sc made Fig. 6d)***; repreat from ★ around.

Fig. 6a

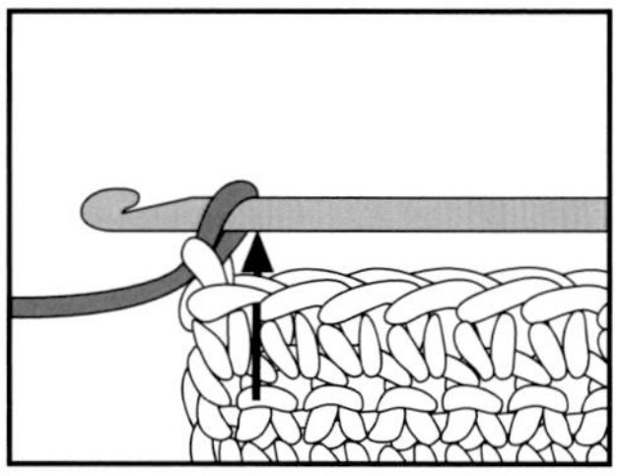

Fig. 6b

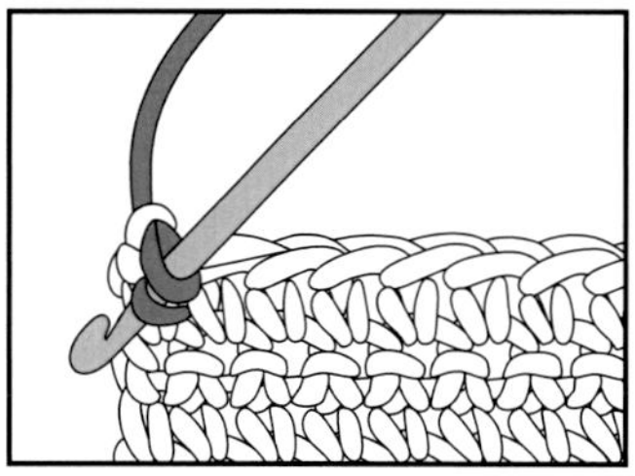

Fig. 6c

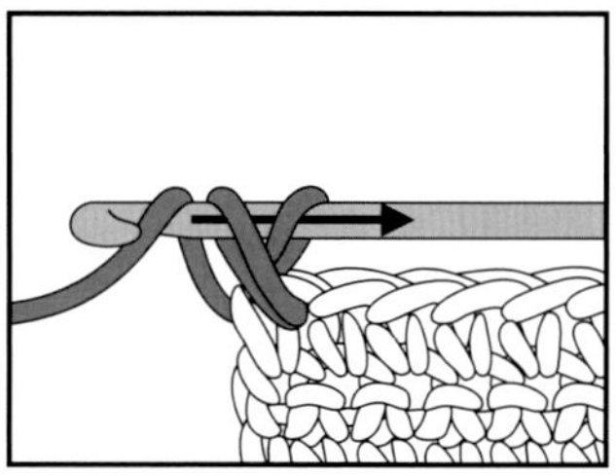

Fig. 6d

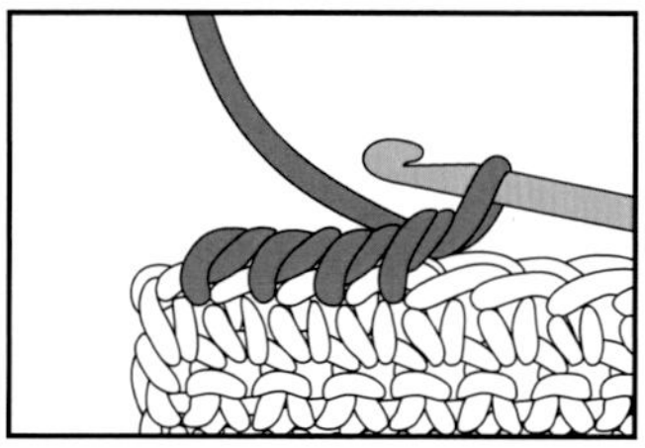

WHIPSTITCH

P1ace two pieces with wrong sides together Sew through bothe pieces oce to secure the beginning of the seam, leving amP1e yarn end to weave in later. Insert the needle from front to back through first stitch and pull yarn theough ***(Fig.7)***, ★ insert the needle from front to back through next stitch and pull yarn through; repeat from ★ across.

Fig. 7

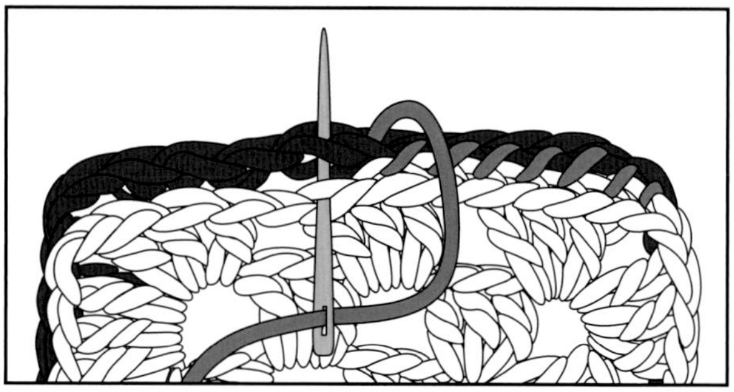

FRINGE

Cut a piece of Cardboard 3" wide and $^1/_2$" longer than you want your finished fringe to be. Wind the yarn **loosely** and **evenly** around the cardboard lengthwisr until the card is filled, then cutacross one end; repeat as needed.

Hold together half as many strands of yarn as desired for the finished fringe; fold in half.

With **wrong** side facing and using a crochet hook, draw the folded end up through a stitch or space and pull the loose ends through the folded end ***(Figs. 8a & c)***; draw the knot up **tightly** ***(Figs. 8b & d)***. Repeat, spacing as desired.

Lay flat on a hard surface and trim the ends.

Fig.8a

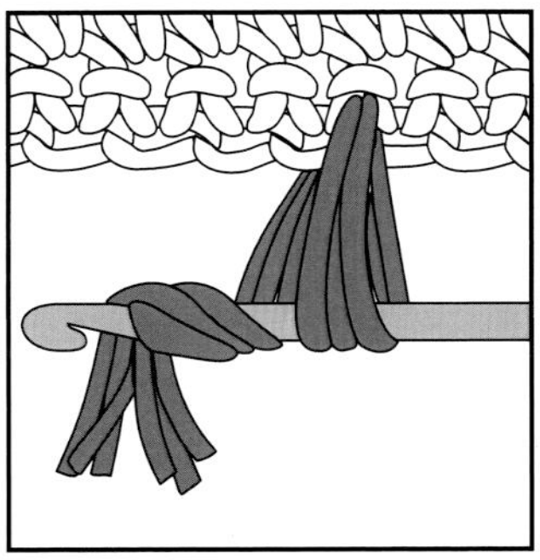

Fig. 8b

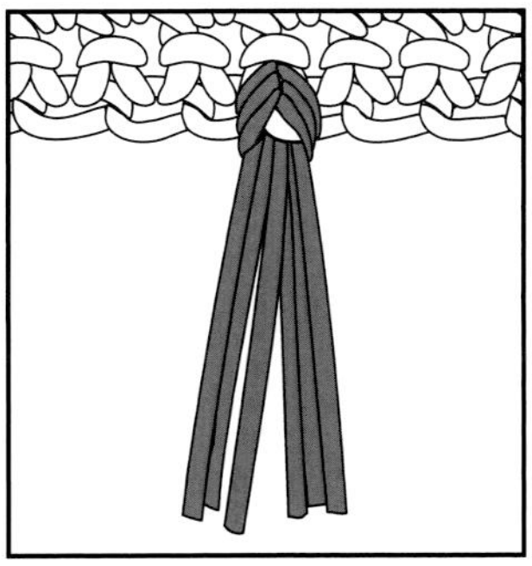

Fig.8c

Fig. 8d

Afghans made and instructions tested by Jennie Black, Pam Bland, Mike Cates, Helga Christensen, June Clevenger, Lisa Hightower, Carol McElroy, Dale Potter, Rondi Rowell, Donna Sc=oelliner, Bill Tanner, Carol Thompson,Lee Tribett, and Augustine Zajac.

Made in U.S.A.

Fisherman's Comfort

To Crochet

Finished Size: 52" x 71"

MATERIALS

Worsted Weight Yarn:
71 ounces, (2,020 grams, 4,465 yards)
Crochet hook, size I (5.50 mm) or size needed for gauge

GAUGE: 13 sc and 14 rows = 4"

Ch 60 **loosely**.

Rnd 1 (Right side**):** Sc in second ch from hook and in each ch across to last ch, 3 sc in last ch; working in free loops of beginning ch ***(Fig. 1, page 4)***, sc in next 57 chs, 2 sc in same st as first sc; join with slip st to first sc: 120 sc.

Note #1: Work in Back Loops Only throughout ***(Fig. 2, page 4)***, unless otherwise indicated.

Note #2: To work Front Post double crochet (abbreviated FPdc), YO, insert hook from front to back around post of st indicated, YO and pull up a loop ***(Fig. 3, page 4)***, (YO and draw through 2 loops on hook) twice.

Rnd 2: Ch 1, 2 sc in same st, † sc in next 7 sc, work FPdc around next sc ***(Figs. 4a & b, page 4),*** (sc in next 13 sc, work FPdc around next sc) 3 times, sc in next 7 sc, 3 sc in next sc †, sc in next sc, 3 sc in next sc, repeat from † to † once, sc in last sc and in same st as first sc; join with slip st to first sc: 128 sts.

Rnds 3-8: Ch 1, 2 sc in same st, † sc in each sc across to next FPdc, (work FPdc around next FPdc, sc in each sc across to next FPdc) across to last FPdc **before** next corner 3-sc group, work FPdc around last FPdc †, (sc in each sc across to center sc of next corner 3-sc group, 3 sc in center sc) twice, repeat from † to † once, sc in each sc across to center sc of next corner 3-sc group, 3 sc in center sc, sc in each sc across and in same st as first sc; join with slip st to first sc: 176 sts.

To work Cluster, YO, insert hook in **both** loops of next st, YO and pull up a loop, YO and draw through 2 loops on hook, ★ YO, insert hook in **same** st, YO and pull up a loop, YO and draw through 2 loops on hook; repeat from ★ 3 times **more**, YO and draw through all 6 loops on hook ***(Figs. 4a & b, page 5)***.

Rnd 9: Ch 1, 2 sc in same st, † (work Cluster, sc in each sc across to next FPdc) across to last FPdc **before** next corner, ★ work Cluster, sc in each sc across to next corner 3-sc group, work Cluster, 3 sc in center sc †; repeat from ★ once **more**, then repeat from † to † once, work Cluster, sc in each sc across to last sc, work Cluster, sc in same st as first sc; join with slip st to first sc: 184 sts.

Rnd 10: Ch 1, 2 sc in same st, ★ sc in each st across to center sc of next corner 3-sc group, 3 sc in center sc; repeat from ★ 2 times **more**, sc in each st across and in same st as first sc; join with slip st to first sc: 192 sc.

Rnd 11: Ch 1, 2 sc in same st, sc in next 2 sc, † work FPdc around next sc, sc in next sc, work Cluster, sc in next 9 sc, work Cluster, sc in next sc †, repeat from † to † across to within 2 sc of next corner 3-sc group, work FPdc around next sc, ★ sc in next 2 sc, 3 sc in center sc, sc in next 2 sc, repeat from † to † across to within 2 sc of next corner 3-sc group, work FPdc around next sc; repeat from ★ 2 times **more**, sc in each sc across and in same st as first sc; join with slip st to first sc: 200 sts.

Rnd 12: Ch 1, 2 sc in same st, ★ † sc in each sc across to next FPdc, (work FPdc around next FPdc, sc in each st across to next FPdc) across to last FPdc before next corner 3-sc group, work FPdc around last FPdc †, sc in each sc across to center sc of next corner 3-sc group, 3 sc in center sc; repeat from H 2 times **more**, then repeat from † to † once, sc in each sc across and in same st as first sc; join with slip st to first sc: 208 sts.

Rnd 13: Ch 1, 2 sc in same st, sc in each sc across to next FPdc, † work FPdc around next FPdc, sc in next 3 sc, work Cluster, (sc in next 2 sc, work Cluster) twice, sc in next 3 sc †, repeat from † to † across to last FPdc before next corner 3-sc group, work FPdc around last FPdc, ★ sc in each sc across to center sc of next corner 3-sc group, 3 sc in center sc, sc in each sc across to next FPdc, repeat from † to † across to last FPdc before next corner 3-sc group, work FPdc around last FPdc; repeat from ★ 2 times **more**, sc in each sc across and in same st as first sc; join with slip st to first sc: 216 sts.

Rnds 14-22: Repeat Rnd 12, 9 times: 288 sts.

Rnd 23: Ch 1, 2 sc in same st, work Cluster, ★ † sc in each sc across to next FPdc, (work Cluster, sc in each sc across to next FPdc) across to last FPdc before next corner 3-sc group, work Cluster, sc in each sc across to next corner 3-sc group, work Cluster †, 3 sc in center sc, work Cluster; repeat from ★ 2 times **more**, then repeat from † to † once, sc in same st as first sc; join with slip st to first sc: 296 sts.

Rnds 24-91: Repeat Rnds 10-23, 4 times; then repeat Rnds 10-21 once **more**: 840 sts.

Rnd 92: Ch 1, working from left to right, work reverse sc in both loops of each st around ***(Figs. 5a-d, page 5)***; join with slip st to first st, finish off.

Design by John H . Fedderson Jr.

Log Cabin

To Crochet

Finished Size: 50" x 57"

MATERIALS

Medium Weight Yarn:
- MC (Tan) - 13$^1/_2$ ounces, (380 grams, 850 yards)
- Color A (Maroon) - 4 ounces, (110 grams, 250 yards)
- Color B (Blue) - 3$^1/_2$ ounces, (100 grams, 220 yards)
- Color C (Lt Blue) - 3$^1/_2$ ounces, (100 grams, 220 yards)
- Color D (Brown) - 4$^1/_2$ ounces, (130 grams, 280 yards)
- Color E (Green) - 7 ounces, (200 grams, 440 yards)
- Color F (Lt Green) - 7 ounces, (200 grams, 440 yards)

Crochet hook, size I (5.50 mm) or size needed for gauge

Yarn needle

GAUGE: Each Block = 11" x 12"

BLOCK (Make 20)

With Color A , ch 7 **loosely**.

Row 1 (Right side)**:** Sc in third ch from hook and in next 4 chs: 5 sc.

Note: Loop a short piece of yarn around any stitch to mark Row 1 as **right** side.

Row 2: Ch 2, turn; skip first sc, sc in next 4 sc and in next ch.

Note: Begin working in rounds.

To work **treble crochet *(abbreviated tr)***, YO twice, insert hook in st or sp indicated. YO and pull ua a loop, (YO and draw throough 2 loops on hook) 3 times.

Rnd 1: Ch 4 **(counts as first tr, now and throughout)**, turn; dc in same st and in next 4 sc, (dc, tr, ch 1, tr, dc) in next ch, skip next ch; working in free loops of beginning ch ***(Fig. 2b, page 4)***, (dc, tr, ch 1, tr, dc) in first ch, dc in next 4 chs, (dc, tr, ch 1, tr, dc) in next ch, (dc, tr) in same st as first tr, ch 1; join with slip st to first tr: 24 sts and 4 ch-1 sps.

Rnd 2: Ch 3 **(counts as first dc, now and throughout)**, do **not** turn; dc in next 7 sts, (dc, tr, ch 1, tr, dc) in next ch-1 sp, P1ace marker around last ch-1 made for joining P1acement, dc in next 4 sts, (dc, tr, ch 1, tr, dc) in next ch-1 sp, dc in next 8 sts, (dc, tr, ch 1, tr, dc) in next ch-1 sp, dc in next 4 sts, (dc, tr, ch 1, tr, dc) in last ch-1 sp; join with slip st to first dc, finish off: 40 sts and 4 ch-1 sps.

Rnd 3: With **wrong** side facing, join Color B with slip st in marked corner ch-1 sp; ch 4, dc in same sp and in each st across to next corner ch-1 sp, † (dc, tr, ch 1, tr, dc) in corner ch-1 sp, dc in each st across to next corner ch-1 sp †, (dc, tr) in corner ch-1 sp, drop Color B ***(Fig. 1 , page 4)***, with Color C, YO and draw through, (tr, dc) in same sp, dc in each st across to next corner ch-1 sp, repeat from † to † once, (dc, tr) in same sp as first tr, sc in first tr to form last ch-1 sp: 56 sts and 4 ch-1 sps.

Rnd 4: Ch 4, turn; dc in same sp and in each st across to next corner ch-1 sp, † (dc, tr, ch 1, tr, dc) in corner ch-1 sp, dc in each st across to next corner ch-1 sp †, (dc, tr) in corner ch-1 sp, cut Color C, with Color B, YO and draw through, (tr, dc) in same sp, dc in each st across to next corner ch-1 sp, repeat from † to † once, (dc, tr) in same sp as first tr, ch 1, P1ace marker around last ch-1 made for joining P1acement; join with slip st to first tr, finish off: 72 sts and 4 ch-1 sps.

Rnds 5 and 6: Repeat Rnds 3 and 4 with Color D and MC: 104 sts and 4 ch-1 sps.

Rnds 7 and 8: Repeat Rnds 3 and 4 with Color E and Color F: 136 sts and 4 ch-1 sps.

Rnd 9: With right side facing, join MC with slip st in marked corner ch-1 sp; ch 4, dc in same sp and in each st across to next corner ch-1 sp, ★ (dc, tr, ch 1, tr, dc) in corner ch-1 sp, dc in each st across to next corner ch-1 sp; repeat from ★ around, (dc, tr) in same sp as first tr, ch 1; join with slip st to first tr, finish off.

ASSEMBLY

Using P1acement Diagram as a guide for color position, P1ace two Blocks with wrong sides together. Using MC and working through inside loops only, whipstitch Blocks together ***(Fig. 7, page 6)***, forming 4 vertical strips of 5 Blocks each, beginning in first corner ch and ending in next corner ch; whipstitch strips together in same manner.

PLACEMENT DIAGRAM

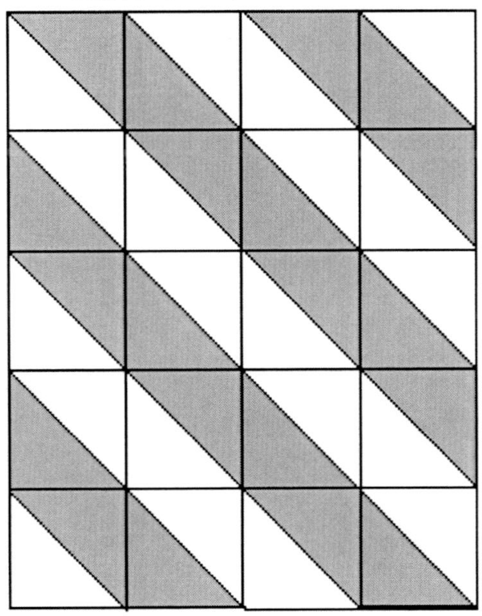

EDGING

With right side facing, join MC with slip st in any corner ch-1 sp; ch 3, dc in next tr and in each st, sp, and joining across to next corner ch-1 sp, ★ (dc, ch 1, dc) in corner ch-1 sp, dc in each st, sp, and joining across to next corner ch-1 sp; repeat from ★ around, dc in same sp as first dc, ch 1; join with slip st to first dc, finish off.

Design by Nancy Fuller.

Buffalo Check Afghan

To Crochet

Finished Size: 46$^{1}/_{2}$" x 65$^{1}/_{2}$" (118 cm x 166.5 cm)

MATERIALS

Medium Weight Yarn:
Color A (Black) - 35 ounces, 2,200 yards
(990 grams, 2,012 meters)
Color B (Teal) - 35 ounces, 2,200 yards
(990 grams, 2,012 meters)
Crochet hook, size K (6.50 mm) **or** size needed for gauge

Note: Entire Afghan is worked holding two strands of yarn together.

GAUGE: In pattern, 9 sts and 8 rows = 4" (10 cm)

Gauge Swatch: 4" (10 cm) square
Ch 11 **loosely**.
Work same as Afghan for 8 rows.

Note #1: Afghan is worked from side to side.

Note #2: When joining yarn and finishing off, leave a 9" (23 cm) end to be worked into fringe.

With Color A, ch 149 **loosely**.

Row 1 (Right side)**:** Dc in fourth ch from hook and in next ch, (ch 3, skip next 3 chs, dc in next 3 chs) across: 24 ch-3 sps.

Note: Loop a short piece of yarn around any stitch to mark Row 1 as **right** side.

Row 2: Ch 3, turn; skip first 3 dc, working over next ch-3 **and** in skipped chs of beginning ch, dc in next 3 chs, ch 3, ★ skip next 3 dc, working over next ch-3 **and** in skipped chs of beginning ch, dc in next 3 chs, ch 3; repeat from★ across to last 3 sts, skip next 2 dc, slip st in last st; finish off: 25 ch-3 sps.

Row 3: With **right** side facing and working over slip st, join Color B with slip st in first st one row **below**; ch 3, working over next ch-3, dc in next 2 dc one row **below**, ★ ch 3, skip next 3 dc, working over next ch-3, dc in next 3 dc one row **below**; repeat from ★ across: 24 ch-3 sps.

Row 4: Ch 3, turn; skip first 3 dc, working over next ch-3, dc in next 3 dc one row **below**, ch 3, ★ skip next 3 dc, working over next ch-3, dc in next 3 dc one row **below**, ch 3; repeat from ★ across to last 3 sts, skip next 2 dc, slip st in last st; finish off: 25 ch-3 sps.

Row 5: With **right** side facing and working over slip st, join Color A with slip st in first st one row **below**; ch 3, working over next ch-3, dc in next 2 dc one row **below**, ★ ch 3, skip next 3 dc, working over next ch-3, dc in next 3 dc one row **below**; repeat from ★ across: 24 ch-3 sps.

Row 6: Ch 3, turn; skip first 3 dc, working over next ch-3, dc in next 3 dc one row **below**, ch 3, ★ skip next 3 dc, working over next ch-3, dc in next 3 dc one row **below**, ch 3; repeat from ★ across to last 3 sts, skip next 2 dc, slip st in last st; finish off: 25 ch-3 sps.

Repeat Rows 3-6 until Afghan measures approximately 46$^{1}/_{2}$" (118 cm) from beginning ch, ending by working Row 5; do **not** finish off.

Last Row: Turn; slip st in first 3 dc, working over next ch-3, dc in next 3 dc one row **below**, slip st in next 3 sts ★ working over next ch-3, dc in next 3 dc one row **below**, slip st in next 3 sts; repeat from ★ across; finish off.

Add additional fringe across short edge of Afghan ***(Figs. 8a & b, page 7)***.

Add fringe to opposite edge of Afghan.

Design by Carole Prior .

Cedar Lake

To Knit

Finished Size: Approximately 46" x 69"

MATERIALS

Worsted Weight Yarn, approximately:
44 ounces, (1,250 grams, 2,890 yards)
31" Circular knitting needle, size 15 (10.00 mm)
or size needed for gauge Cable needle

GAUGE: Working double strand, in Stockinette Stitch,
11 sts and 14 rows = 4"

Note: See Yarn Overs ***(Figs. 5a-d, page 5)***.

Holding 2 strands of yarn together, cast on 130 sts.

Row 1: (K1, P1) across.

Row 2: (P1, K1) across.

Rows 3-9: Repeat Rows 1 and 2, 3 times; then repeat Row 1 once more.

To work Cable (uses next 4 sts), slip 2 sts onto cable needle and hold in back of work, K2 from left needle, K2 from cable needle.

Row 10 (Right side)**:** P1, (K1, P1) 3 times, KS, (P2, work Cable) twice, † P4, K2, K2 tog, YO, (KS, K2 tog, YO) 3 times, K3, P4 †, work Cable, P2, work Cable, repeat from † to † once, (work Cable, P2) twice, K4, (P1, K1) 4 times.

To work purl 2 together through the back loops (abbreviated P2 tog tbl), insert the right needle into the back of both sts from back to front ***(Fig. 9)*** and purl them together.

Fig. 9

Row 11: K1, (P1, K1) 3 times, PS, (K2, P4) twice, † K4, P1, P2 tog tbl ***(Fig. 9)***, YO, P1, YO, P2 tog, (P2, P2 tog tbl, YO, P1, YO, P2 tog) 3 times †, P1, K4, P4, K2, P4, repeat from † to † once, P1, K4, P4, (K2, P4) twice, (K1, P1) 4 times.

Row 12: P1, (K1, P1) 3 times, KS, (P2, work Cable) twice, † P4, (K2 tog, YO, K3, YO, slip 1, K1, PSSO) 4 times, P4 †, work Cable, P2, work Cable, repeat from † to † once, (work Cable, P2) twice, K4, (P1, K1) 4 times.

Row 13: K1, (P1, K1) 3 times, PS, (K2, P4) twice, K4, P28, K4, P4, K2, P4, K4, P 28, K4, P4, (K2, P4) twice, (K1, P1) 4 times.

Row 14: P1, (K1, P1) 3 times, KS, (P2, work Cable) twice, † P4, (YO, slip 1, K1, PSSO, KS) 4 times, P4 †, work Cable, P2, work Cable, repeat from † to † once, (work Cable, P2) twice, K4, (P1, K1) 4 times.

Row 15: K1, (P1, K1) 3 times, PS, (K2, P4) twice, † K4, (YO, P2 tog, P2, P2 tog tbl, YO, P1) 4 times, K4 †, P4, K2, P4, repeat from † to † once, P4, (K2, P4) twice, (K1, P1) 4 times.

Row 16: P1, (K1, P1) 3 times, KS, (P2, work Cable) twice, † P4, K2,
YO, slip 1, K1, PSSO, K2 tog, YO, (K3, YO, slip 1, K1, PSSO, K2 tog, YO) 3 times, K1, P4 †, work Cable, P2, work Cable, repeat from † to † once, (work Cable, P2) twice, K4, (P1, K1) 4 times.

Row 17: K1, (P1, K1) 3 times, PS, (K2, P4) twice, K4, P 28, K4, P4, K2, P4, K4, P 28, K4, P4, (K2, P4) twice, (K1, P1) 4 times.

Rows 18-225: Repeat Rows 10-17, 26 times.

Row 226: (P1, K1) across.

Row 227: (K1, P1) across.

Rows 228-234: Repeat Rows 226 and 227, 3 times; then repeat Row 226 once **more**.

Bind off all sts in pattern.

Design by Lee Tribett.

FLYING GEESE

To Knit

Finished Size: Approximately 45" x 60"

MATERIALS

Worsted Weight Yarn, approximately:
- MC (Tan) - 25 ounces, (710 grams, 1,760 yards)
- CC (Colors A-G)
  - Color A (Red) - 3 ounces, (90 grams, 205 yards)
  - Color B (Green) - 3 ounces, (90 grams, 205 yards)
  - Color C (Lt. Green) - 3 ounces, (90 grams, 205 yards)
  - Color D (Black) - 3 ounces, (90 grams, 205 yards)
  - Color E (Gold) - 3 ounces, (90 grams, 205 yards)
  - Color F (Brown) - 3 ounces, (90 grams, 205 yards)
  - Color G (Lt. Brown) - 3 ounces, (90 grams, 205 yards)
- Straight knitting needles, size 8 (5.00 mm) or size needed for gauge

Yarn needle

Note: Each repeat (Rows 2-33) uses approximately 13 yards of CC.

GAUGE: Rows 1-32 = 3½"
Each Strip = 7½" wide

Note: When instructed to slip a stitch, always slip as if to **purl** with yarn held **loosely** on **wrong** side of work.

STRIP (Make 6)

With MC, cast on 37 sts.

Row 1 (Wrong side): Knit across.

Note #1: Following Chart, make Strips using color indicated.

Note #2: Carry yarn not being used loosely along edge.

Rows 2 and 3: With CC, K4, slip 1, (K1, slip 1) 6 times, K3, slip 1, (K1, slip 1) 6 times, K4.

Rows 4 and 5: With MC, K 17, slip 1, K1, slip 1, K 17.

Rows 6 and 7: With CC, K4, slip 1, (K1, slip 1) 5 times, K7, slip 1, (K1, slip 1) 5 times, K4.

Rows 8 and 9: With MC, K 15, slip 1, (K1, slip 1) 3 times, K 15.

Rows 10 and 11: With CC, K4, slip 1, (K1, slip 1) 4 times, K 11, slip 1, (K1, slip 1) 4 times, K4.

Rows 12 and 13: With MC, K 13, slip 1, (K1, slip 1) 5 times, K 13.

Rows 14 and 15: With CC, K4, slip 1, (K1, slip 1) 3 times, K 15, slip 1, (K1, slip 1) 3 times, K4.

Rows 16 and 17: With MC, K 11, slip 1, (K1, slip 1) 7 times, K 11.

Rows 18 and 19: With CC, K4, slip 1, (K1, slip 1) twice, K 19, slip 1, (K1, slip 1) twice, K4.

Rows 20 and 21: With MC, K9, slip 1, (K1, slip 1) 9 times, K9.

Rows 22 and 23: With CC, K4, slip 1, K1, slip 1, K 23, slip 1, K1, slip 1, K4.

Rows 24 and 25: With MC, K7, slip 1, (K1, slip 1) 11 times, K7.

Rows 26 and 27: With CC, K4, slip 1, K 27, slip 1, K4.

Rows 28 and 29: With MC, KS, slip 1, (K1, slip 1) 13 times, KS.

Rows 30 and 31: With CC, knit across; cut CC.

Rows 32 and 33: With MC, knit across. Rows 34-545: Repeat Rows 2-33, 16 times. Bind off all sts.

CHART

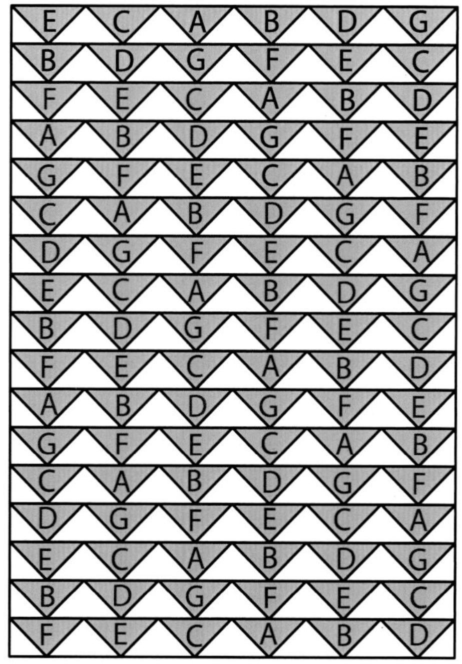

With MC and using Chart as a guide for P1acement, weave Strips together as follows:

With **right** side of two Strips facing you and edges even, sew through both sides once to secure the seam. Insert the needle under bottom bar of first ridge on right Strip and pull the yarn through ***(Fig. 10)***. Insert the needle under the top bar of the next ridge on the left Strip.

Repeat from side to side being careful to match the rows.

Fig. 10

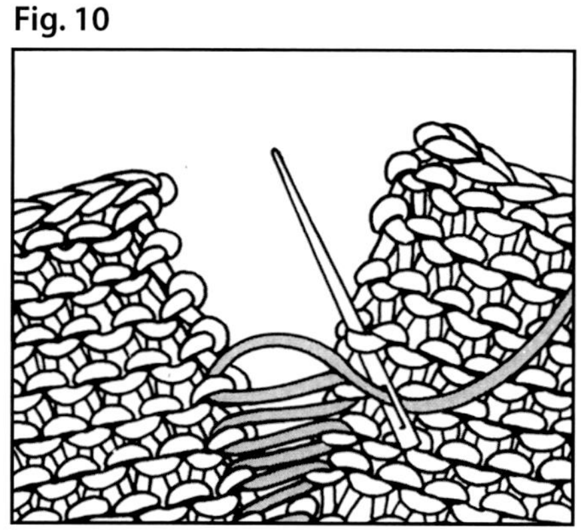

Add fringe ***(Figs. 8c & d, page 7)***.

Design by Gail Tanquary.

DEER RUN

To Crochet

Finished Size: Approximately 45" x 59"

MATERIALS

Worsted Weight Yarn, approximately:
- Color A (Green) - 16 ounces, (450 grams, 1,005 yards)
- Color B (Teal) - 12 ounces, (340 grams, 755 yards)
- Color C (Brown) - 10½ ounces, (300 grams, 660 yards)

Crochet hook, size J (6.00 mm) or size needed for gauge

GAUGE: 12 dc and 6 rows = 4"

Note: Due to the nature of this pattern, we suggest you practice the pattern stitch by working several swatches. It may be necessary to pull up the initial loop slightly higher when working the center FPdc, and then adjusting as necessary for the preceding and the remaining FPdc. Refer to photo as a guide if necessary.

With Color A, ch 137 **loosely**.
Row 1 (Right side): Dc in fourth ch from hook **(3 skipped chs count as first dc)** and in each ch across: 135 dc.

Note: Loop a short piece of yarn around any stitch to mark last row as right side.

Rows 2-6: Ch 3 **(counts as first dc, now and throughout)**, turn; dc in next dc and in each dc across.

Finish off.

Row 7: With **right** side facing, join Color C with slip st in first dc; ch 1, sc in same st and in next 3 dc, ★ † FPdc around next dc ***(Figs. 4a & b, page 5)***, work FPdc around next dc one row **below**, work FPdc around next dc 2 rows **below**, work FPdc around next dc 3 rows **below**, work FPdc around next dc 2 rows **below**, work FPdc around next dc one row **below**, work FPdc around next dc t, sc in next 5 de; repeat from ★ 9 times **more**, then repeat from † to † once, sc in last 4 dc.

Row 8: Ch 3, turn; dc in next 3 sc and in next 7 skipped dc, (dc in next 5 sc and in next 7 skipped de) across to last 4 sc, dc in last 4 sc; finish off: 135 dc.

Row 9: With **right** side facing, join Color B with slip st in first dc; ch 3, dc in next dc and in each dc across.

Rows 10-14: Ch 3, turn; dc in next dc and in each dc across.

Finish off.

Row 15: With **right** side facing, join Color C with slip st in first dc; ch 1, sc in same st and in next 3 dc, ★ † work FPdc around next dc, work FPdc around next dc one row **below**, work FPdc around next dc 2 rows **below**, work FPdc around next dc 3 rows **below**, work FPdc around next dc 2 rows **below**, work FPdc around next dc one row **below**, work FPdc around next dc †, sc in next 5 dc; repeat from ★ 9 times more, then repeat from † to † once, sc in last 4 dc.

Row 16: Ch 3, turn; dc in next 3 sc and in next 7 skipped dc, (dc in next 5 sc and in next 7 skipped dc) across to last 4 sc, dc in last 4 sc; finish off: 135 dc.

Row 17: With **right** side facing, join Color A with slip st in first dc; ch 3, dc in next dc and in each dc across.

Repeat Rows 2-17 until Afghan measures approximately 58" from beginning ch, ending by working Row 7; do **not** finish off.

EDGING

Ch 3, do not turn; dc evenly around working 3 dc in each corner; join with slip st to first dc, finish off.

Design by Marion Miedema.

MOUNTAIN TRAILS

To Crochet

FINISHED SIZE: Approximately 48" X 71"

MATERIALS
Worsted Weight Yarn, approximately:
MC (Burgundy) - 26 ounces,
(740 grams, 1,785 yards)
Color A (Natural) - 17 ounces,
(480 grams, 1,195 yards)
Color B (Green) - 2 ounces,
(60 grams, 135 yards)
Crochet hooks, sizes H (5.00 mm) **and** I (5.50 mm) **or** sizes needed for gauge

GAUGE: One repeat from point to point = 6"
and 7 rows = 4¼"

Gauge Swatch: (12" x 4¼")
With smaller size hook, ch 50 loosely.
Work same as Afghan for 7 rows.

To dc decrease, ★ YO, insert hook in **next** st or sp YO and pull up a loop, YO and draw through 2 loop on hook· repeat from ★ once **more** YO and draw through all 3 loop on hook **(counts as one dc)**.

With MC and smaller size hook, ch 206 **loosely**.

Row 1 (Right side)**:** Dc in third ch from hook and in next 9 chs, (dc ch 3 dc) in next ch dc in next 9 chs, dc decrease, ★ skip next 3 chs dc decrease, dc in next 9 chs (dc ch 3, dc) in next ch dc in next 9 chs, dc decrease; repeat from ★ across: 176 dc.

Note: Loop a short piece of yarn around any stitch to mark last row as **right** side.

Rows 2-4: Ch 2 turn· dc in next 10 dc, (dc ch 3, dc) in next ch-3 sp dc in next 9 dc, ★ dc decrease twice, dc in next 9 dc (dc ch 3 dc) in next ch-3 sp, dc in next 9 dc; repeat from ★ across to last 2 dc, dc decrease.

Finish off.

Row 5: With **right** side facing and smaller size hook Jom Color A with slip st in first dc; ch 2, dc in next 10 dc, (dc, ch 3, dc) in next ch-3 sp, dc in next 9 dc, ★ dc decrease twice, dc in next 9 dc, (dc, ch 3, dc) in next ch-3 sp, dc in next 9 dc; repeat from ★ across to last 2 dc, dc decrease.

Rows 6 and 7: Repeat Rows 2 and 3.

Finish off.

To **sc decrease**, pull up a loop in next 2 sts, YO and draw through all 3 loops on hook **(counts as one sc)**.

Row 8: With **wrong** side facing and larger size hook, join MC with slip st in first dc; ch 1, pull up a loop in same st and in next dc, YO and draw through all 3 loops on hook, ch 1, skip next dc, (sc in next de, ch 1, skip next dc) 4 times, (sc, ch 3, sc) in next ch-3 sp, ch 1, (skip next dc, sc in next dc, ch 1) 4 times, ★ skip next dc, sc decrease twice, ch 1, skip next dc, (sc in next dc, ch 1, skip next dc) 4 times, (sc, ch 3, sc) in next ch-3 sp, ch 1, (skip next dc, sc in next dc, ch 1) 4 times; repeat from ★ across to last 3 dc, skip next dc, sc decrease; finish off: 88 sps.

Row 9: With **right** side facing and larger size hook, join Color B with slip st in first sc; ch 1, pull up a loop in same st and in next ch-1 sp, YO and draw through all 3 loops on hook, ch 1, (sc in next ch-1 sp ch 1) 4 times, (sc, ch 3 sc) in next ch-3 sp, ch 1, ★ (sc in next ch-1 sp ch 1) 10 times, (sc, ch 3 sc} in next ch-3 sp, ch 1• repeat from ★ across to last 5 ch-1 sps (sc in next ch-1 sp ch 1) 4 times pull up a loop in next ch-1 sp and in last st, YO and draw through all 3 loops on hook; finish off: 95 sps.

Row 10: With **wrong** side facing and larger size hook, join MC with slip st in first st; ch 1, pull up a loop in same st and in next ch-1 sp, YO and draw through all 3 loops on hook ch 1 (sc in next ch-1 sp, ch 1) 4 times, (sc ch 3 sc) in next ch-3 sp ch 1, ★ (sc in next ch-1 sp, ch 1) 5 times, skip next ch-1 sp, (sc in next ch-1 sp, ch 1) 5 times, (sc, ch 3, sc) in next ch-3 sp, ch 1; repeat from ★ across to last 5 ch-1 sps, (sc in next ch-1 sp, ch 1) 4 times, pull up a loop in next ch-1 sp and in last st, YO and draw through all 3 loops on hook; finish off.

Row 11: With **right** side facing and larger size hook, join Color A with slip st in first st, ch 1, pull up a loop in same st and in next ch-1 sp YO and draw through all 3 loops on hook, ch 1, (sc in next ch-1 sp, ch 1) 4 times, (sc, ch 3, sc) in next ch-3 sp ch 1, ★ (sc in next ch-1 sp, ch 1) 5 times skip next ch-1 sp, (sc in next ch-1 sp, ch 1) 5 times, (sc, ch 3, sc) in next ch-3 sp, ch 1; repeat from ★ across to last 5 ch-1 sps, (sc in next ch-1 sp, ch 1) 4 times, pull up a loop in next ch-1 sp and in last st, YO and draw through all 3 loops on hook; do **not** finish off.

Change to smaller size hook.

Row 12: Ch 2, turn; dc in first ch-1 sp and in next sc, (dc in next ch-1 sp and in next sc) 4 times, (dc ch 3, dc) in next ch-3 sp, ★ dc in next sc, (dc in next ch-1 sp and in next sc) 4 times, dc decrease, skip next ch-1 sp, dc decrease, dc in next sc, (dc in next ch-1 sp and in next sc) 4 times, (dc, ch 3, dc) in next ch-3 sp dc in next sc; repeat from ★ across to last 5 ch-1 sps, (dc in next ch-1 sp and in next sc) 4 times, dc decrease; finish off.

Row 13: With right side facing and smaller size hook, join MC with slip st in first dc; ch 2, dc in next 10 dc, (dc, ch 3, dc) in next ch-3 sp, dc in next 9 dc, ★ dc decrease twice, de in next 9 dc, (dc, ch 3, dc) in next ch-3 sp, dc in next 9 dc; repeat from ★ across to last 2 dc, dc decrease.

Rows 14-16: Repeat Rows 2-4.

Rows 17-136: Repeat Rows 5-16, 10 times.

Design by Mary Lamb Becker.

EVERGREEN RETREAT

To Crochet

Finished Size: Approximately 54" x 74"

MATERIALS

Worsted Weight Yarn, approximately:
Color A (Dark Tea!) - 23 ounces, (650 grams, 1,445 yards)
Color B (Tea!) - 23 ounces, (650 grams, 1,445 yards)
Color C (Rust) - 12 ounces, (340 grams, 755 yards)
Crochet hook, size J (6.00 mm) or size needed for gauge

GAUGE: 12 sc and 13 rows = 4"

LONG EXTENDED SINGLE CROCHET
(abbreviated Long ex sc)

Insert hook in sc on row indicated **below** next sc, YO and pull up a loop, insert hook in Back Loop Only of sc, YO and draw through st **and** first loop on hook ***(Fig. 11a)***, YO and draw through both loops on hook ***(Fig. 11b)*** **(Long Extended Single Crochet made).**

Fig. 11a

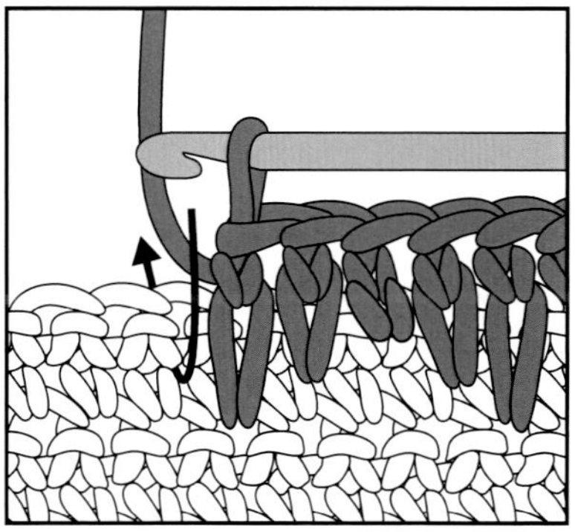

Fig. 11b

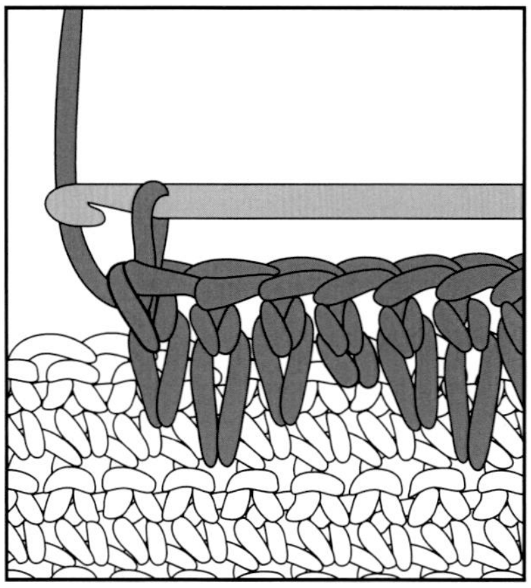

With Color A, ch 60 loosely.

Rnd 1 (Right side)**:** Sc in second ch from hook and in each ch across to last ch, 3 sc in last ch; working in free loops of beginning ch ***(Fig. 2b, page 4)***, sc in next 57 chs, 2 sc in same st as first sc; join with slip st to first sc: 120 sc.

Note #1: loop a short piece of yarn around any stitch to mark last round as **right** side.

Note #2: Work in Back loops Only throughout ***(Fig. 3, page 5)***, unless otherwise indicated.

Rnd 2: Ch 1, 2 sc in same st, sc in next 57 sc, 3 sc in next sc, sc in next sc, 3 sc in next sc, sc in next 57 sc, 3 sc in next sc, sc in next sc and in same st as first sc; join with slip st to first sc: 128 sc.

Rnds 3-7: Ch 1, 2 sc in same st, (sc in each sc across to center sc of next corner 3-sc group, 3 sc in center sc) 3 times, sc in each sc across and in same st as first sc; join with slip st to first sc: 168 sc.

Finish off.

Rnd 8: With **right** side facing, join Color C with slip st in same st as joining; ch 1, 2 sc in same st, ★ work long ex sc one row **below** ***(Figs. 11a & b)***, † work Long ex sc 2 rows below, work Long ex sc 3 rows **below**, work Long ex sc 2 rows **below**, work Long ex sc one row **below** †, repeat from † to † across to center sc of next corner 3-sc group, 3 sc in center sc; repeat from ★ 2 times more, work long ex sc one row **below**, repeat from † to † across, sc in same st as first sc; join with slip st to both loops of first sc, finish off: 176 sts.

Rnd 9: With **right** side facing and working in both loops, join Color B with slip st in same st as joining; ch 1, 2 sc in same st, (sc in each st across to center sc of next corner 3-sc group, 3 sc in center sc) 3 times, sc in each st across and in same st as first sc; join with slip st to Back loop Only of first sc: 184 sc.

Rnds 10-17: Ch 1, 2 sc in same st, (sc in each sc across to center sc of next corner 3-sc group, 3 sc in center sc) 3 times, sc in each sc across and in same st as first sc; join with slip st to first sc: 248 sc.

Finish off.

Rnd 18: Repeat Rnd 8: 256 sts.

Rnds 19-27: With Color A, repeat Rnds 9-17: 328 sc. Finish off.

Rnds 28-88: Repeat Rnds 8-27, 3 times; then repeat Rnd 8 once **more**; at the end of Rnd 88, do **not** finish off: 816 sts.

Rnd 89: Ch 1, working from **left** to **right**, work reverse sc in both loops of each st around ***(Figs. 6a-d, page 6)***; join with slip st to first st, finish off.

Design by John H. Feddersen Jr.

Camp Blanket

To Crochet

Finished Size: 46" x 62"

MATERIALS

Worsted Weight Yarn:
Scraps - 42 ounces, (1,190 grams, 2,760 yards)
Crochet hook, size I (5.50 mm) or size needed for gauge

GAUGE: In pattern, 15 sts and 9 rows = 4"

Note: Change colors as desired ***(Fig. 2)***.

With first color, ch 174 **loosely**.

Row 1: P1ace marker in first ch from hook to mark ch-1 sp, P1ace marker in fifth ch from hook to mark skipped st, dc in sixth ch from hook, (ch 1, skip next ch, dc in next ch) across: 85 ch-1 sps.

To work **beginning Split treble crochet *(abbreviated beginning Split tr)***. YO, insert hook in first ch-1 sp, YO and pull up a loop (3 loops on hook), insert hook in skipped st one row below ch-1 ***(Fig. 12a)***, YO and pull up a loop (4 loops on hook), insert hook in same ch-1 sp ***(Fig. 12b)***, YO and draw through ch-1 sp **and** 2 loops on hook, YO and draw through 2 loops on hook ***(Fig 12c)***, YO and draw through 2 loops on hook ***(Figs. 12d)*** **(beginning Split tr made)**.

Fig. 12a

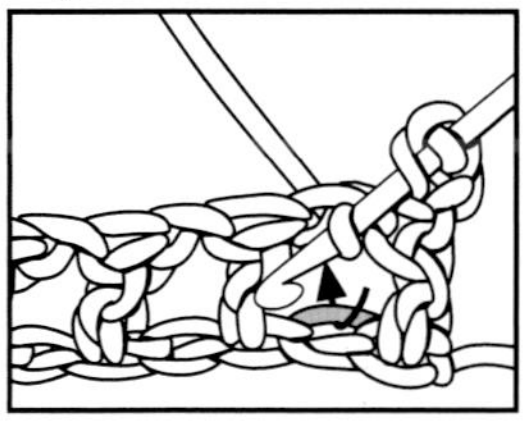

Fig. 12b

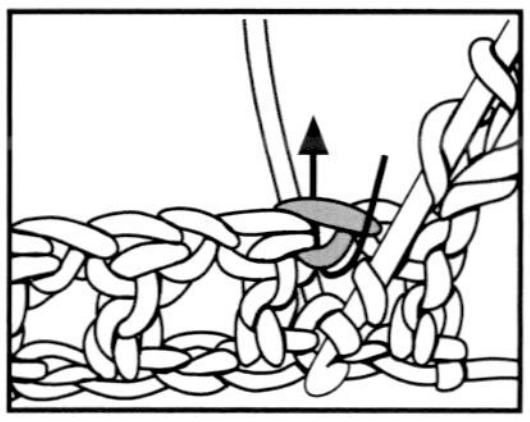

Fig. 12c

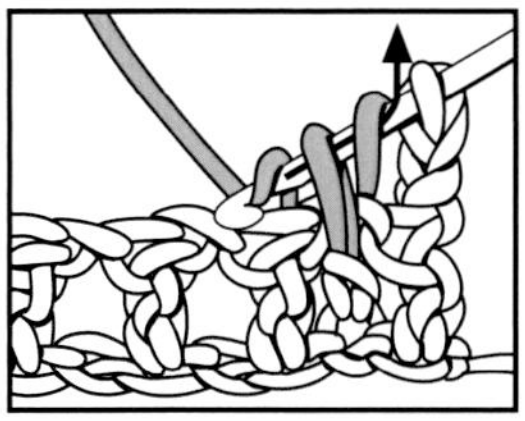

Fig. 12d

To work Split treble crochet **(abbreviated Split tr)**
YO, insert hook in same ch-1 sp, YO and pull up a loop (3 loops on hook), insert hook in skipped st one row **below** ch-1, YO and pull up a loop (4 loops on hook), insert hook in same ch-1 sp, YO and draw through ch-1 sp **and** 2 loops on hook, (YO and draw through 2 loops on hook) twice.

Row 2 (Right side)**:** Ch 3 **(counts as first dc, now and throughout)**, turn; work beginning Split tr, (dc in next ch-1 sp, work Split tr) across to beginning ch, dc in top of beginning ch: 171 sts.

Note: Loop a short piece of yarn around any stitch to mark last row as right side.

Row 3: Ch 4 **(counts as first dc plus ch 1, now and throughout)**, turn; skip next st, dc in next dc, (ch 1, skip next st, dc in next dc) across: 85 ch-1 sps.

Row 4: Ch 3, turn; work beginning Split tr, (dc in next ch-1 sp, work Split tr) across to last dc, dc in last dc: 171 sts.

Repeat Rows 3 and 4 until Afghan measures 59$^{1}/_{2}$" from beginning ch ending by working Row 4.

Finish off.

EDGING

Rnd 1: With right side facing, join yarn with slip st in any corner; ch 1, sc evenly around working 3 sc in each corner; join with slip st to first sc.

Rnds 2-5: Ch 1, sc in each sc around working 3 sc in center sc of each corner; join with slip st to first sc.

Rnd 6: Ch 1, working from **left** to **right**, work reverse sc in each sc around ***(Figs. 6a-d, page 5)***; join with slip st to first st, finish off.

Design by Ingrid Nels.

INDIAN WRAP

TO CROCHET

Finished Size: Approximately 48" x 72"

MATERIALS

Worsted Weight Yarn approximately:
Color A (Black) - 10 ounces,
(280 grams, 655 yards)
Color B (Green) - 13 ounces,
(370 grams, 855 yards)
Color C (Tan) - 16 ounces,
(450 grams 1,050 yards)
Color D (Red) - 16 ounces
(450 grams 1 050 yards)
Crochet hook, size I (5.50 mm) or size needed
for gauge Yarn needle

GAUGE: In pattern and working in Back Loops Only,
13 sc and 14 rows = 4"

PATTERN STITCHES

TREBLE CROCHET ***(abbreviated tr)***

YO twice, insert hook in st indicated, YO and pull up a loop, (YO and draw through 2 loops on hook) 3 times.

DOUBLE TREBLE CROCHET ***(abbreviated dtr)***

YO 3 times, insert hook in st indicated, YO and pull up a loop, (YO and draw through 2 loops on hook) 4 times.

Note #1: Afghan is worked from side to side.

Note #2: When joining yarn and finishing off, leave a 9" length to be worked into fringe.

PANEL (Make 2)

With Color A, ch 234 **loosely.**

Row 1 (Right side)**:** Sc in second ch from hook and in each ch across; finish off: 233 sc.

Note #1: Loop a short piece of yarn around any stitch to mark last row as **right** side.

Note #2: Work in Back Loops Only throughout ***(Fig. 3, page 5)***, unless otherwise indicated.

Rows 2 and 3: With **right** side facing join Color B with sc in first sc ***(see Joining With Sc, page 4)***; sc in each sc across; finish off.

Row 4: With **right** side facing, join Color C with sc in first sc; sc in each sc across; finish off.

Row 5: With **right** side facing, join Color A with sc in first sc; sc in each sc across; finish off.

Rows 6 and 7: With **right** side facing, join Color D with sc in first sc; sc in each sc across; finish off.

Row 8: With **right** side facing, join Color C with sc in first sc; sc in each sc across; finish off.

Rows 9 and 10: With **right** side facing, join Color B with sc in first sc; sc in each sc across; finish off.

Row 11: With **right** side facing, join Color C with sc in first sc; sc in each sc across· finish off.

Rows 12 and 13: With **right** side facing, join Color D with sc in first sc; sc in each sc across; finish off.

Row 14: With **right** side facing, join Color A with sc in first sc; sc in each sc across; finish off.

Row 15: With **right** side facing, join Color B with sc in first sc; sc in next 29 sc, ★ † dc in free loop of sc one row **below** next sc ***(Fig. 2a page 4)***. skip sc behind dc **(now and throughout)**, tr in free loop of sc 2 rows **below** next sc, skip sc behind tr **(now and throughout)**, dtr in free loop of sc 3 rows **below** next sc, skip sc behind tr **(now and throughout)**, tr in free loop of sc 2 rows **below** next sc, dc in free loop of sc one row **below** next sc † sc in next 19 sc; repeat from ★ 6 times **more**, then repeat from † to † once, sc in last 30 sc; finish off.

Row 16: With **right** side facing, join Color B with sc in first sc; sc in each st across; finish off.

Row 17: With **right** side facing join Color D with sc in first sc; sc in next 4 sc, (dc in free loop of sc one row below next sc, sc in next 5 sc) across; finish off.

Row 18: With **right** side facing join Color D with sc in first sc· sc in next 5 sts, dc in free loop of sc one row **below** next sc sc in next 3 sc dc in free loop of sc one row **below** next sc, ★ sc in next dc, dc in free loop of sc one row **below** next sc, sc in next 3 sc, dc in free loop of sc one row **below** next sc; repeat from ★ across to last 6 sts, sc in last 6 sts; finish off.

Row 19: With **right** side facing, join Color D with sc in first sc; sc in next 6 sts, dc in free loop of sc one row **below** next sc, sc in next sc. dc in free loop of sc one row **below** next sc, ★ sc in next 3 sts, dc in free loop of sc one row **below** next sc, sc in next sc, dc in free loop of sc one row **below** next sc; repeat from ★ across to last 7 sts sc in last 7 sts; finish off.

Row 20: With **right** side facing, join Color A with sc in first sc; sc in next 7 sts, de in free loop of sc one row **below** next sc, (sc in next 5 sts de in free loop of sc one row **below** next sc) across to last 8 sts sc in last 8 sts; finish off.

Row 21: With **right** side facing, join Color D with sc in first sc; sc in next 6 sc, dc in free loop of dc one row **below** next sc sc in next dc, dc in free loop of dc one row **below** next sc, ★ sc in next 3 sc dc in free loop of dc one row **below** next sc, sc in next dc, dc in free loop of dc one row **below** next sc; repeat from ★ across to last 7 sc, sc in last 7 sc- finish off.

Row 22: With **right** side facing, join Color D with sc in first sc; sc in next 5 sc, dc in free loop of st one row **below** next sc, sc in next 3 sts dc in free loop of sc one row **below** next sc, ★ sc in next sc, dc in free loop of sc one row **below** next sc sc in next 3 sts dc in free loop of sc one row **below** next sc, repeat from ★ across to last 6 sc sc in last 6 sc: finish off.

Row 23: With **right** side facing, join Color D with sc in first sc; sc in next 4 sc (dc in free loop of sc one row below next sc, sc in next 5 sts) across; finish off.

Row 24: With **right** side facing, join Color B with sc in first sc; sc in next 23 sts, ★ † dc in free loop of dc one row **below** next sc, tr in free loop of dc 2 rows **below** next sc, dtr in free loop of dc 3 rows **below** next sc, tr in free loop of dc 2 rows **below** next sc, dc in free loop of dc one row **below** next sc †, sc in next 7 sts; repeat from ★ 14 time **more**, then repeat from † to † once, sc in last 24 sts; finish off.

Row 25: With **right** side facing, join Color B with sc in first sc; sc in each st across; finish off.

Row 26: With **right** side facing, join Color C with sc in first sc; sc in next 4 sc, (dc in free loop of sc one row **below** next sc, sc in next 5 sc) across; finish off.

Row 27: With **right** side facing, join Color C with sc in first sc; sc in next 5 sts, dc in free loop of sc one row **below** next sc, sc in next 3 sc, dc in free loop of sc one row **below** next sc, ★ sc in next dc, dc in free loop of sc one row **below** next sc, sc in next 3 sc, dc in free loop of sc one row **below** next sc; repeat from ★ across to last 6 sts, sc in last 6 sts; finish off.

Row 28: With **right** side facing, join Color C with sc in first sc; sc in next 6 sts, dc in free loop of sc one row below next sc, sc in next sc, dc in free loop of sc one row below next sc ★ sc in next 3 sts dc in free loop of sc one row below next sc sc in next sc dc in free loop of sc one row below next sc; repeat from ★ across to last 7 sts, sc in last 7 sts; finish off.

Row 29: With **right** side facing, join Color A with sc in first sc; sc in next 7 sts, dc in free loop of sc one row **below** next sc, (sc in next 5 sts, dc in free loop of sc one row **below** next sc) across to last 8 sts, sc in last 8 sts· finish off.

Row 30: With right side facing, join Color C with sc in first sc; sc in next 6 sc dc in free loop of dc one row below next sc sc in next dc, dc in free loop of dc one row below next sc, ★ sc in next 3 sc, dc in free loop of dc one row below next sc, sc in next dc, dc in free loop of dc one row below next sc; repeat from ★ across to last 7 sc sc in last 7 sc; finish off.

Row 31: With **right** side facing, join Color C with sc in first sc; sc in next 5 sc dc in free loop of sc one row **below** next sc, sc in next 3 sts, dc in free loop of sc one row **below** next sc, ★ sc in next sc, dc in free loop of sc one row **below** next sc, sc in next 3 sts, dc in free loop of sc one row **below** next sc; repeat from★across to last 6 sc, sc in last 6 sc; finish off.

Row 32: With **right** side facing join Color C with sc in first sc; sc in next 4 sc, (dc in free loop of sc one row **below** next sc, sc in next 5 sts) across· finish off.

Row 33: With right side facing, join Color B with sc in first sc; sc in next 29 sts, ★ † dc in free loop of dc one row below next sc tr in free loop of dc 2 rows below next sc dtr in free loop of de 3 rows below next sc tr in free loop of dc 2 rows below next sc, dc in free loop of dc one row below next sc † sc in next 19 sts; repeat from ★ 6 times more, then repeat from † to † once, sc in last 30 sts; finish off.

Rows 34-83: Repeat Rows 16-33 twice, then repeat Rows 16-29 once more.

ASSEMBLY

With Color A and working through both loops, whipstitch Panels together matching last rows ***(Fig. 7, page 6)***.

Add additional fringe ***(Figs. 8a & b, page 7)***.

Design by Irma Park.

Winter Blocks Afghans

shown on page 27

To Crochet

Finished Size: 48" x 61"

MATERIALS

Worsted Weight Yarn:
- Ecru - 43 ounces, (1,220 grams, 2,825 yards)
- Brown - 9 ounces, (260 grams, 615 yards)
- Tan - 25 yards
- Green - 55 yards
- Black - 15 yards

Crochet hook, size H (5.00 mm) or size needed for gauge
Tapestry needle
Yarn needle

GAUGE: In pattern, (sc, ch 1) 9 times and
17 rows = 4"
Each Block with Edging = 12"w x 12¼"

BLOCK (Make 24)

With Ecru, ch 54 **loosely**.

Row 1 (Right side)**:** Sc in second ch from hook, (ch 1, skip next ch, sc in next ch) across**:** 26 ch-1 sps.

Note: Loop a short piece of yarn around any stitch to mark Row 1 as right side.

Row 2: Ch 1, turn; sc in first sc and in next ch-1 sp, (ch 1, skip next sc, sc in next ch-1 sp) across to last sc, sc in last sc: 25 ch-1 sps.

Row 3: Ch 1, turn; sc in first sc, (ch 1, skip next sc, sc in next ch-1 sp) across to last sc, sc in last sc: 26 ch-1 sps.

Rows 4-25: Repeat Rows 2 and 3, 11 times.

Row 26: Ch 1, turn; sc in first sc and in next ch-1 sp, (ch 1, skip next sc, sc in next ch-1 sp) 13 times, P1ace marker around last ch-1 made to mark center, (ch 1, skip next sc, sc in next ch-1 sp) across to last sc, sc in last sc: 25 ch-1 sps.

Row 27: Repeat Row 3.

Rows 28-51: Repeat Rows 2 and 3, 11 times.
Finish off.

EDGING

To work **Long Single Crochet *(abbreviated Long sc)***, insert hook in ch-1 sp 2 row below on 2 sts below now or st indicated ***(Fig. 13)***, YO and pull up a loop even with last st made, YO and pull up a loop even with last st made, YO and draw through both loops on hook.

Fig. 13

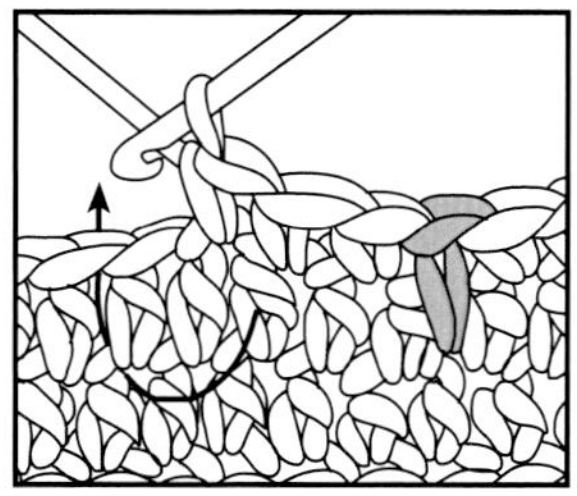

With **right** side facing, join Color A with slip st in last sc on Row 51; † working in end of rows, skip first 3 rows, work (Long sc, ch 1) twice in next row, ***(Fig. 13)***, (skip next row, work Long sc in next row, ch 1) 21 times, skip next row, work (Long sc, ch 1, Long sc) in next row, skip next 3 rows †, slip st in free loop of first ch, ***(Fig. 2b, page 4)*** skip next 2 chs; working over beginning ch, work (Long sc, ch 1) twice in next ch-1 sp, (skip next ch, work Long sc in next ch-1 sp, ch 1) 22 times, skip next ch, work (Long sc, ch 1, Long sc) in next ch-1 sp, skip next 2 chs, slip st in free loop of next ch, repeat from † to † once; working across last row, slip st in first sc, skip next ch-1 sp and next sc, (work Long sc, ch 1) twice in next ch-1 sp, (skip next sc, work Long sc in next ch-1 sp, ch 1) 22 times, skip next sc, work (Long sc, ch 1, Long sc) in next ch-1 sp, skip next sc and next ch-1 sp; join with slip st to first slip st, finish off.

FINISHING

CROSS STITCH

Add cross stitch design to each Block ***(Fig. 14)***, following Charts, page 32. Each square on the Chart represents one cross stitch. Each cross stitch is worked over a center ch-1 sp into ch-1 sps around the center ch-1 sp. To center design, use marked ch-1 on Block matched to center st on Chart. Using yarn needle and long strand of yarn doubled, weave end under several stitches on back of piece to secure (do not tie knot). With **right** side facing and Row 51 of Block at top, work cross stitches as follows: bring needle up at 1, down at 2 (half cross made), up at 3, down at 4 **(cross stitch completed, Fig. 14)**. All cross stitches should cross in the same direction. Finish off by weaving end under several stitches on back; cut close to work.

Following Charts, add designs to Blocks as follows:
3 Bears, 3 Deer, 4 Moose, and 10 Trees.

Fig. 14

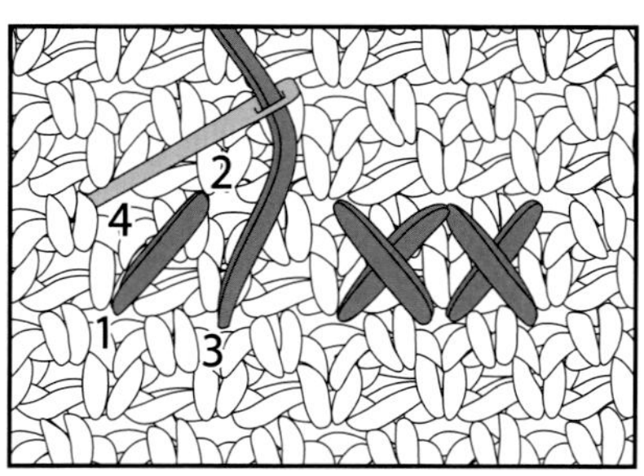

ASSEMBLY

With Brown, using Placement Diagram as a guide, and working through inside loops only, whipstitch 5 complete Blocks into 4 vertical strips ***(Fig. 7, page 6)***, beginning in slip st of first corner and ending in slip st of next corner; whipstitch strips together in same manner.

EDGING

With **right** side facing and working in ch-1 sps, join Color A with slip st in any ch-1 sp; ch 1, working from **left** to **right**, work reverse sc evenly around ***(Figs. 6a-d, page 6)***; join with slip st to first sc, finish off.

ASSEMBLY DIAGRAM

T	M	T	B
D	T	M	T
T	M	T	D
B	T	M	T
T	D	T	B

KEY
T - Tree
M - Moose
B - Bear
D - Deer

CHARTS KEY
- Brown
- Tan
- Green
- Black

BEAR (B)

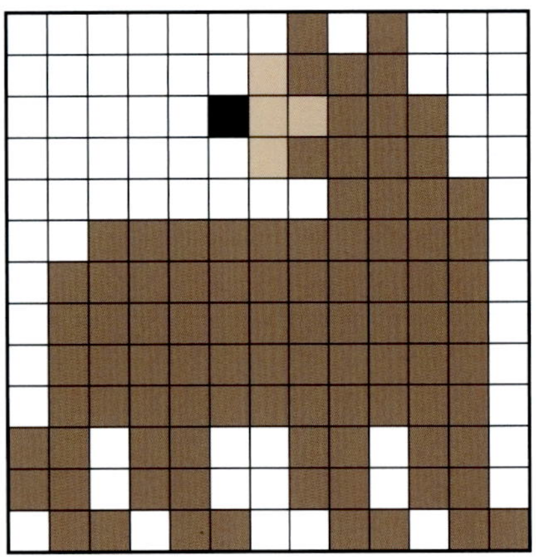

DEER (D)

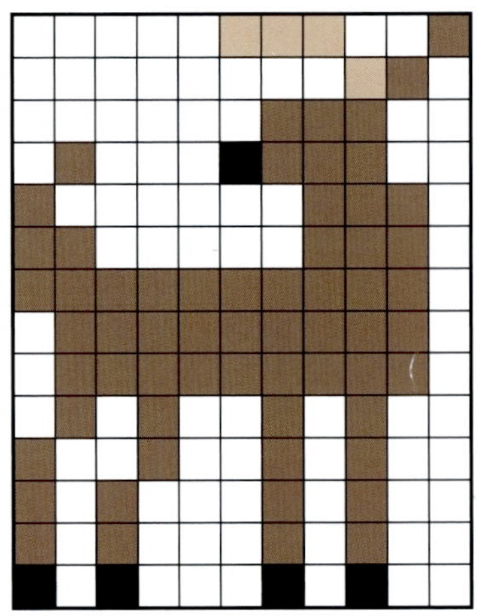

MOOSE (M)

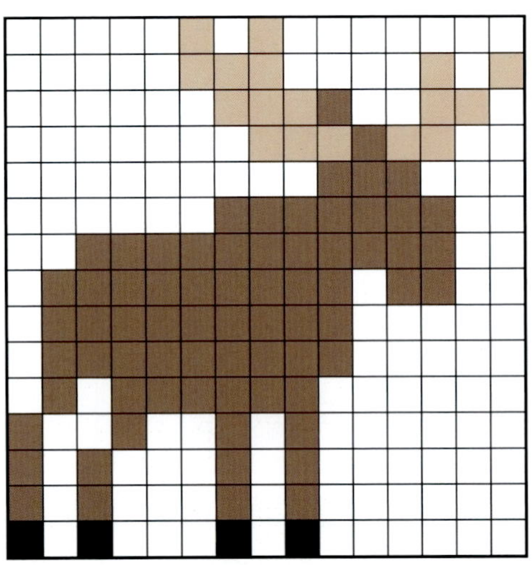

TREE (T)

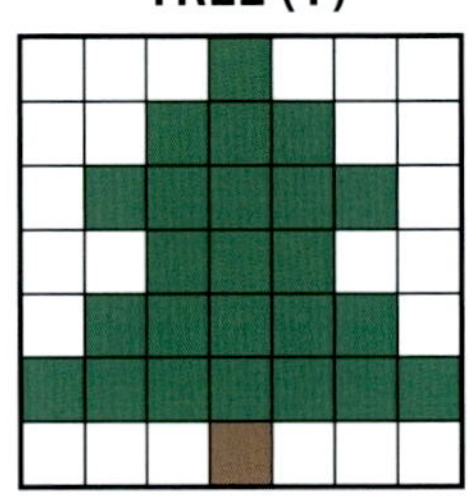